Also by Barbara Siegel Carlson

Books

What Drifted Here
Once in Every Language
Take Five (with four other poets)
Fire Road

Chapbooks

Between the Hours
Between this Quivering

Translations

Open: Selected Poems and Thoughts of Srečko Kosovel (Slovene, with Ana Jelnikar)
Look Back, Look Ahead: Selected Poems of Srečko Kosovel (Slovene, with Ana Jelnikar)

Anthology

A Bridge of Voices: Contemporary Slovene Poetry and Perspectives (ebook, co-edited with Richard Jackson)

CURRENT

Poems by

Barbara Siegel Carlson

LILY POETRY REVIEW BOOKS

CURRENT

Copyright © 2026 by Barbara Siegel Carlson
Published by Lily Poetry Review Books
223 Winter Street
Whitman, MA 02382

https://lilypoetryreview.blog/

ISBN: 978-1-957755-62-5

Cover painting: "The Monk by the Sea," Caspar David Friedrich (1774-1840).
courtesy of Old National Gallery, State Museum Berlin

For Larry, Emmett, Lily and Lizzy

CONTENTS

The Godhead is broken like bread. We are the pieces.
Herman Melville

I

There's an unsolvable part that holds us faltering.
                                        Killarney Clary

CARRYING MY ABYSS

after Adonis

It is the age of clouds of the whitest white
and the lightest blanket you cannot see through.
Your eyelids grow heavy and your dust sparks,
but you cannot hear my voice. You cannot touch
my face thrumming with the age dissolved,
with the minds that have nowhere to turn.
Everything is reflection, illusion, mirage.
You are time without an answer, the age of clouds
always coming together and separating. One
a colossal mouse, another a dragon with a blue snout.
A woman painting in silence who dreams the living and dying
breed in heavenly camps. Her children need
a real bed and warm arms—they're stained
with the sorrow that rises from the dirty streets
and bleeding mouths. While someone is searching
for the whitest white, another discovers the blackest black
is a space on the body where the woman would
wear a dress. As in every room a corner that never ends
stealing the light, eating it, never letting it go.
Does that light disappear? It's like a wind,
an invisible flame in your loins, a divine voice
whose sound leaves no trace—When the young
dreamer lay dying in his sleeping bag
in the rusted bus, his mother heard him
calling in her dream. When Joan of Arc grew
invisible in the flames, where did her spirit go?

REFUGE

My mother painted a colorful jungle
on the upstairs balcony. A deer, bear,
lion, elephant, wolf, lamb and birds
looking at me as they flapped.
The Garden of Eden, she said, and let me
paint the black spots in each animal's eyes.

She called the spots holes
for the soul to pass through, but I saw only
how a tear left a trail down her face.
The grass in the yard yellowed, remained uncut
and blew in rivulets I would dance through
in bare feet, making a tunnel
to a hidden room of grass
my cheek could press into
as the leaves fell.
The clouds blanketed me with a damp scent
after the kids said I had the cooties.

In a tree hollow I found a piece of wood
and called it Adam. I sang to it
as I did to the clouds and the coal-blue
eyes of the tiger that stared down
from the mountainside just before
it started running toward me, then disappeared
at the moment I awoke, heart rising to the siren
that rang past my window.

The house wavered and breathed.
I saw my mother's baby, the one
who died without a name, and my father
who'd survived the war, but whose silence
about the camp became the spray

of sparks and shriek of the train
that struck him when I was too young
to remember. When I asked where
he went, my mother said he was crossing,
and something flashed out her eye,
clear as the eye of the Adam-stick,
the tiger and lamb that held me
transfixed, lost in my bed.

Today I found a half-broken egg
along the road with the unborn bird
still alive, the tiny pink arm
trying to claw its way out. It is
so thin between worlds—the one
in my hands so light
it is nothing I can ever touch.

BLESSING A STONE

Stones along the dirt road shine
in quiet hues at dawn.
Their colors deepen
as the smell of light
revives on the moist road.
I pick one up and rub
the striations, as if I could draw
from the lines some message,
some memory of its passage.
Pausing, I close my eyes
and see the stars. I can almost
reach through the light
and dark particles that hold all I am
to know where I'm going.

FOR WHEN HEATHCLIFF LAY DOWN BY THE OPEN WINDOW DURING A STORM

He began as a rustle in the stove.
Later I felt a rip in my pillow
where feathers spilled out from a pigeon,
a moor-cock, a lapwing. I placed them
on the sill, recalling a nest
of tiny skeletons I found one autumn dawn
after the black of a moonless night
had risen from the heather hills
where trails through the upland
have no borders or vision, only voices
that seep through the windows and walls,
voices that sound in unknown tongues
and reverberate in a mind
whose raptures and terrors blaze
through the cosmos seeking
another body, another life—
and that hunger, that hunger drives
through us in all directions at once.
I found my soul in the emptiness
when the wind and rain ran down his chest.

A MOMENT IN ROME

On a chilly gray morning I step out of my hotel. I go without a map,
turning to a woman in an orange headscarf who sits near the corner
with a cup in front of her, waving to everyone who passes. Further on,
another woman, in an open doorway, smiles through her missing teeth.
Who am I to walk by? *And what can I do?* What does the man holding
an apple, talking into the air, making his way through the middle
of his life, do with me as he walks by? The sparrows are sharing
a few crumbs. Women in burqas stare out from a curve in the road,
their faces unlit, their heads like bells ringing all around, though traffic
drowns them out. The Romans too tried to murder their ghosts.
Where are the souls of those early Christians who were sick, poor
and held only to their faith, their bodies dissolved in the catacombs?
Or the souls of the Jews forced to live where the river overflowed,
or those hoarded into trucks to be taken to the camps? What about
those who shouted or were silenced, violated, condemned, forgiven,
or not, or those who fell down before their captors, forgiving them,
holding out hope and love beyond their death after those who buried
them, those who saved only themselves. Or those who saved nothing
for themselves? Who pass over us now, watching through the clouds
or along the street? Who dwell within me whose voice is mute?

THE FOG IS ADRIFT

Not unafraid of the Taliban takeover.
Waiting for what happens through the bars and veils.

What about the whale that washed up on the private beach?
They couldn't find anyone to rid the stench.

Still we smile at the red boots on the big furry dog, turn our heads away
from the man with bare stumps where his feet should be.

We go by way of the wood, each of us an inscrutable world heating up,
compressing to petrified rock.

Who can imagine the last notes of the whale's song?

Stirring the trees, the wind rubs each leaf, the tree buried in moss, a stick pointing the way
to the valley hidden in a froth of clouds.

The eyelash I couldn't find kept poking my eye. Each lash plucked
leaves an indiscernible hole.

In the sleep of the homeless, the drifter goes on unheard,
deep in our pockets, the forgotten still breathe.

MARKING THE PLACE

She comes with a notebook and pen to sit on a bench on a hill. It's November, midday. She's alone in a foreign country. But not really alone. People live in the valley, only she can't see them. She writes in her notebook. A breeze sends a shiver through the reddish weeds. She hears the tower bell gong 12 times. After the 12th gong she takes a black napkin out of her pocket. There's a stain in the corner. She's not sure where the napkin came from or who she was with, or if she will ever come here again. She puts it on a blank page in her notebook like the wind she has no words for.

FROM A BENCH ON A HILL

—the earthquake of '76, Fagagna, Italy

It still holds the tremors.
The dogs that keep barking,
the man who keeps mowing his grass,
the stranger who rests here.

The village bell tolls for those
who do not hear it anymore
and those who remember when Earth bellowed out
and felt it in their stomach as the dark snow
loosed and the rock poured down.

Whoever rises from my seat has a faint
view of those who lived in the valleys
whose spirits come to the bell tower
and pathways as the evening
turns the color of plum.

Let her look at the jagged blue range in the distance—
and know it crumbles. And the cypresses
that come to a vertical point,
and the mulberry trunks that hold inscrutable
faces in their knots and crevices.

Somewhere the deaf girl wakes
beside her freshly-picked pink
flowers strewn across her pillow
and hears a nightjar trill.

My legs, my back, my empty seat hold traces
of what follows the cries and echoes
between the bell chimes, where you too
might linger and hear

the sound of a fiddle, though the strings
broke. Or notice
the persimmons all lighted
with fruit. Or press a hawthorn berry
between your fingers. The juice is light
as the eyes of the old couple who often sit here
while blackbirds circle the castle remains.

ASIDE THE TRACKS

Just past Zagorje, there's an old pink house
by a family graveyard and a line
of purple snowdrops. Who planted them?
The red squirrel with a tail
like a ghostly feather leaps
over hillocks of air.
Snow-colored mountains
lift the spirit. Mountains hold
hidden paths and abandoned nests.
The tracks pass by a wilderness
of broken windows, shadows
of roofless mansions
all crushed together
like centuries of lives
pressed in the rocks
to be worn away by the wind and water,
a blinding drop here and there.

TO THE STATUES OF ROME

Within your worn stone faces
looking both ways on the bridge
over the Tiber, the hollow
of your chest, skeletal angel
in the St. Peter-in-Chains Church,

and the eyes of you, saint
in the Basilica of Santa Maria Maggiore
that one might beg for release,

while the Gregorian chant went on
in one of the side rooms,
and the tones of *Ave Maria* rose
from another to the dome

and through the Colosseum's gargantuan
matrix, such hammerings and lamentations
emanating and surrounding, such voices carrying

at the same time from street corners and piazzas,
rising, resonating even from the middle
of fountains, though your rough
torsos, pocked arms, gouged cheeks
and chipped lips
told me nothing, nothing. I followed

the green-flamed parrot
flitting through the bare limbs
of a plane tree along the river
as it searched for its food.

HIDDEN NOTE

The fireman believed my doll
in the smoke-filled crib was alive.
Once I dreamt of falling through
a burning floor, till I came
to the neighbor's porch
and stood there watching
my house sail into the night sky.
Now, when a gray flake
from the woodstove floats out
and lands on my shoe, I can't tell
where it came from. It quivers
like the tiny feather I saved.

ELEGY FOR A SCRAP

Where did the scrap of paper come from
to land here on this rug,
its feathery fiber stranded
from what seed to bloom
into sapling and leaf
that opened when a mother gave birth,
the child laid warm
and wet at her breast?
Long after the tree was cut open,
the sap oozed, seeping into the ground.
While the tissue was pressed into paper,
light left the heart

of seven year old Yusof
who, after eating a banana
and kissing his father
goodbye, was found in the rubble.
And 20 year old Shira
whose name means song.
And 30 year old Lurin who went
to take a shower, pray and rest.
"Struck while praying," her fiancé said.

Each scrap reveals an unseen world
when it appears at a moment
like the lady's slipper
hidden in the woods
that looks like a human form, its leaves
like outstretched arms, its blossom
a dark and secret perfume, sprouted
from the forest of ashes, voices and stars.

In a dream I was rapping
on my father's door.
But it was bolted.
When I looked down
I saw a hole in my chest
where so many scraps have vanished,
and one was trying to sing.

II

It's the heart that creates the invisible.

Duo Duo, translated by Lucas Klein

TO THE WIND

What is this wind who takes hold
of my heart and lifts it into the air,
lowers and then lifts it into the air?

Carlos Sahagun

You who set the branches swaying
the trunks rocking
as you go on
searching   scouring
the needles and leaves

lifting sand from the hills
riffling grasses and pondwater

What do you hope to find—?

I'm like the dandelion
whitened with seeds
that release one at a time

each
 broken open—to this
other life

SHADOW OF THE UNTOUCHABLE

Standing out along the path in the Public Garden among spit, broken twigs, geese turds, crushed winter berries and patches of dirty snow, a man with a raw unshaven face and red swollen hands reads on a green bench. In front of him a pigeon with a green shimmer on its neck. Just past him, a gray feather is slightly lifting on a step, which leads to the bronze statue of an angel holding a bowl of bread—the crumbs it perpetually holds to cast. A child's glove is propped on a post of the iron gate, its other buried somewhere in the world.

ALPS FROM THE PLANE

No one has walked those snowy pockets
whose jagged peaks pierce the clouds,
while roots have sunk into earth
and vanished like bodies.

In a glass case in Celje,
a five-hundred-year old flayed skin
has no cocoon, no pasture, no sin.
Nameless, without depth, altered

at different frequencies, a presence
we might only perceive when we dream,
see up close or from the sky. At the core it burns.
The afterbirth was once a shelter too.

WITHOUT A NOTE

When I worry about our world, I think of Tu Fu
who lived twenty-five hundred years ago
in a world torn by strife, and fearing for his life,
he fled while his children starved,
and when he returned to his wife
sobbing in her shabby dress
and his young children's faces pale and drawn,
in his grief he unwrapped a small silk blanket
and gave them powder and rouge,
briefly forgetting his journey through a battlefield
where frozen bodies lay in the moonlight.
Now the firefly hides and the cricket
is silent and brown as ancient skin.
A few leaves cling to the trees
holding a life that has no note
like buds in the silence of winter.

VOICES IN LEAVES

Everything will leave us except the shadows
W.S. Merwin

When the trees first opened their leaves
and began to speak he was a child
alone in the rustlings
and when the geese clamored just overhead
he followed their calls
to the edge of a field
wondering about the brother he never knew
tucked in his mother's gaze
when she looked out the window
close to the old trees
he was drawn to their voices
their vast ranges
mysterious as his own
hushed in a language of shadows
he followed them wondering
how we cast ourselves
not knowing one from another
as the shadows all mingled

LESSENING

I think you would have liked
that I lay *All of It Singing* down
in the wet grass to tie my shoe
this foggy morning on the bog
amid the slight stir of the rusted
needles on a pine branch, turning
to your poems again as I walk
into my own blind spaces, the splash
of the frog too quick to see, water
ringing into nothing I can follow.
The heron's just taken off, rasping
because I've come too close.
Something's in the fallen haze.
A silk tent wavers in the weeds, a shelter
that traps what it can. Overhead
the swan sounds like the hinges
of a swing a child is pumping
to a place where "The soul barks,
the soul meows" under, over and
through the call of the dove
and the ache to be lifted
by a feather on the road.

A FOREST REMNANT

Along the bog path I find you,
wooden figure with a fin
for a wing, your face
worn away, or maybe
you're a totem
carved and rubbed
by grit and ash,
water and wind.
Once you swayed
with your kind,
then broke and
scraped along
before coming to the spot
far from your tree
where I behold you
wordless as a prayer
to the missing
with a pale sheen
on your grayish brown
lightweight body,
something so still
and holy that came
to me in human form
like a face on the water.

GLIMPSES

The early morning webs tremble—
the catches must be good.
Between the weeds
these holy eyes—hundreds—
no, thousands—of broken and unbroken
threads the creator has cast.

New path, and a new corridor
past some dry animal droppings on a stone
to a small picnic table set on bare ground.
Someone had a small fire here recently.

Water so still it looks like the sky
with a shadowy fringe of pines.
In stillness
there's no boundary

but an opening—
hard to tell, as between
a woman's legs—that infinite place—
geese cry through the fog and this
whiteness of water traceless
as a prayer given
to love, to birth—& then—
for there—

FOR THE ONE WITH AN EMPTY HAND

"We meet at the touch of infinite worlds,"
these were the words that came from a dream,
and I felt as though I were handed a pearl,

but I'd like to know why it makes my head whirl,
and why this longing to understand is as keen
as my love for the fairy house I made as a girl,

the phenomena of a wind-filled world
hidden under twigs and leaves, unseen
till I lay down to watch the walls unfurl

through the breeze where every leaf that twirled
seemed to come from a cloud that gleamed,
while beneath the layers a grain was hurled

through the waves to land in the world
where I was eating a cupcake filled with crème
and walked past a man whose hand had uncurled.

Whatever wind opens the hands of this world
unleashes what can't be changed or redeemed
where we meet at the touch of infinite worlds
where a hand that looks empty holds out a pearl.

COUNTLESS POSSIBILITIES

There was an itch on her back she couldn't scratch,

a voluptuous cloud above every country,

a man far away she could grow wet with.

Spiders leaving their kingdoms in the barbed wires,

abandoned trailers, blackberry brambles, bark of the shaggy oak

& leaves of the red maple like musicians unreeled by their playing.

Like bridges we touch down at either end over our reflections.

Opening the door to the shed with its rusty hinges,

the bee with its sacs of pollen to light the way.

For she who was depleted slept

to be awakened indistinguishable from the dew that reached every blade.

Dangling from a line to cradle the newly fallen.

To be a handful of drops that keeps one alive, resounding chimes.

A body of light without a country, blushed nubs before they open.

To be the flowing inside every eye that never stops channeling

each tiny click part of the mint, with sun warming the hush

that rises from every ravine where a body has lain,

fated to wander like a crystal in the memory of Earth.

TAKEN

Why has her train stopped
in the middle of the woods
where a neon-vested worker
stands in a patch of light?

She whispered "I love you"
to the one she could no longer see,
wondering if somehow
she could feel him from wherever
he was now despite the broken
branches strewn along the track.

There was something else she wanted
to tell him about the hike
where they saw some ancient
trees no one had ever climbed
and lit water surged
over the rocks below.

Her foot almost slipped—why
did she say nothing—then?
Maybe he feels a rumbling, a slight
vibration in his chest
too, as in the forest
out the window

a solitary branch stirs
hidden among the rest
till a ray of sun holds it for a moment
as though it is all there is.

CLOUDSCAPE

Massive and illusory
roadless and singular
your contours constantly
changing, separating
into islands, archipelagos—

each burning coal
a body of hidden waters,
history and breath
tinged with red
and streaks of violet,

my eyes will become your
sapphire holes through being
in unearthly dimension
whose sphere overshadows
this slim shoreline
where I walk between weeds
waving and blushed   illuminated
for a moment at dusk.

THE VISITOR

A black and white pigeon chick was standing in the corner. The scruffy-looking squab's short feathers pressed to its skin.

It looked at me, tilting its head, quivering a little, doing a kind of tap dance on the pavement, moving sideways, slightly to the left, cha-cha-like.

Later on the fourth floor, the same mottled bird appeared all puffed up at the window and blinked at me. It stared, blinking every few seconds.

Sometimes opening its mouth.

Surely it was a sign, leaving me to wonder about why you had gone away in the first place, and whether it was really you who'd left. Or someone from an earlier life.

Every time the bird opened its mouth, it told me something I could almost say.

MOTHER TO A DAUGHTER IN PAIN

In late autumn dusk
a red leaf blazed
amid the tangled
trails of underbrush,
quivering under the trill
of the last crickets whose wings
we never see
as I became you, you
became me, the sepia branch
of a pine coming to life
like a conductor poised
above the red leaf,
drawing it to some higher power,
and holding it
in the stillness of prayer.

CARTOGRAPHER OF LOST ROADS

A pool of shade appeared bottomless.

C.D. Wright

It seemed like she'd come to listen to someone
other than herself. She could've been
a librarian or chicken plant worker
dressed in a skirt. But the other day
when I was walking down a shady road
I came to a dragonfly dangling
from a mailbox post. There was something
eerily transcendent, like the cover photo
of her *Deepstep Come Shining*—
the old woman's chest a brilliant background
for 2 dead hummingbirds hanging from a string
around her neck, her eyes blurry pools
looking elsewhere as though she could hear
"parts of his lonely body" still humming.

GUROV, LATER

The beauty of it is in its hiddenness.

The Lady and the Dog—Chekhov

We are all in cages, scanning the dark sky
for the new moon, a distant light
like the smell of the sea that mingled with us
as we watched the water recede
with its afterglow on the sand.

When I returned to my other life
reading the paper, eating cabbage stew,
while a storm rattled at the window and I spat blood,
and the present filled me with grayness
and disgust, I remembered her kisses, saw her
in the bookshelves, from every corner
breathing, rustling on a stair,
making small footprints beside me.

But then what is memory—what's nostalgia?
Whatever flows through the birch's
blushed fretwork of branches,
the linden limbs' broad tangle?

What remains of the first snow
when in childhood, I pressed my face
to the glass, watching snowflakes
cover the mud-filled street?

Outside, the streets are slushy. A drunk
falls down. Someone hands me
a card that says Pray.
People have lost, faraway looks
on their faces. And yet how close
the moon once seemed,
feeling our bodies rise.

III

Door in the mountain
let me in.

Jean Valentine

HOW MANY ARE BURIED
IN UNMARKED GRAVES?

She dug a small hole in a corner
under a bush, in a patch of dirt
near where no one walked.

Pressed in a candy wrapper,
and over it she gently placed
the piece of glass she'd found.

It glowed like the buttercup
under her brother's chin.

She sprinkled it with sand
and framed it with sticks,
before throwing on more earth.

Then she made a map, starting
from her back door.

LIKE IT WAS YESTERDAY

Fog shrouds the cranberry bog
I walk along, stepping by some weeds
migrants pulled a few days ago.
That day I saw them in their hats
and baggy clothes, bending over
in the sun, and I waved to them.

One of the men rose and walked across
the springy leaf-covered vine work
to say hello. He said he saw me
with my grandchildren the other day,
and they reminded him of his, the ones
he's never met in person.

Then he was telling me
of his escape from Cambodia
over forty years ago, amid the terror
of executions and beheadings,
like it was yesterday. His eyes darkened,
looked far away, then back at me.

Already the weeds have yellowed
and lie there wet on the grassy road.
So quiet now at dawn, but for the geese
that wail through the fog
calling to each other
and me in my dew-soaked shoes.

PATCH OF WOODS

On my walk I was thinking about you
and your last treatment, how parts
of your hands and feet had gone numb.
The bulldozers were gone
from the sandhills, fog filling the trees
that flanked the bogs. Everything up close
stood out, damp tufts of grass
by the bank. As soon as the speckled wet frog
sensed me, it plunked into the water,
leaving the rock of rust-colored pockmarks
and incisions an unreadable relief map,
or a book near a silk hammock
nestled sideways in some wildflowers,
the spider hidden, its hunger invisible
as its reach, like the stars still burning
inside us, ourselves rooted to their power
that pulses unseen. I strayed
off the bog road into a bordering patch
of woods where a spider strand broke
across my cheek, and I couldn't
brush it away, like so much of who we are
that is inconceivable and voiceless.

HIS SIGN ASKS FOR WATER

Joseph can't see where everyone goes each day
and doesn't care where they sleep,
but where they dream when they return
to their night place past this place
on the pavement, where he sits against the wall
and reads. He doesn't need much—his pants
he sews again and again, his Bible's
thin pages of psalms and revelations.
Here he sings in Akan.
Here, too, he sleeps.

When he dreams, the clouds open
to water, a mirror of the purest light
where the shadows disappear.
When the rain comes, he soaks it in.

His skin glows like the man
he once saw in a ring of fire,
consumed by the shrieks into voices
of weaverbirds. After the gang surrounded
the man, Joseph couldn't breathe.
For how long he didn't speak—
still that radiance
has not dissolved but lightened
his bones, and some days he just
disappears, leaving the pavement washed.

RECALLING SIDDHARTHA

Hesse once said he wanted
to be buried with his books
whose words I breathed, despairing

how my son had left
without a word. And did I leave
my lover, or did she leave me?

I called to my father to ask him,
although I knew he would think
my words just ravings
of an old man.

Hesse too rasped like a heron
that lifts its wings
before the one
who comes too close.

Now I stay close to the river,
although my ferryman
long ago crossed

into the voices still
coming from the waves and leaves
that breathe all around.

I CALL YOU

After Sappho 62

You cowered   heart slowing to wood
laurel tree still
in your leaves   everlasting

but everything sweeter   is lighter
than that   of a kiss
and for them   you are no *traveler*
no part of earth

But I scarcely ever
listened to the voice of the *soul*
beloved   of God's eye

You who *got there first:*
beautiful   throughout
I close my eyes

to all I thought
and the clothes you wore

and such leaves that hide
all you are   for *now* I call you
to arrive kindly
as no other

A YOUNG ENGLISH POET LOOKS ON

My grave covered with violet leaves
lies beside Severn's, between the trees.
Severn who kept me alive at the end
after how many friends, even my brother
I believed would care for me, but who left
for America instead. They all kept away,
perhaps out of fear. Only Severn
one autumn day gathered late summer
flowers along the rough road
to Rome, placing them beside me
in the carriage, their moist flower scent
let my spirit blood, making Rome
and Fanny's love eternal,
while part of me stayed *a feather*
on the sea, a mote of sunlight,
a dryad in a tree whose yellow-white eyes
could penetrate the walls of that dark
narrow room where I lay for months,
the carnelian marble she gave me
warm in my hand, my books close by,
as I stared at the ceiling of painted rosettes,
listening to the trickle of water
in the fountain below, waiting
to rise. Her letters went unread,
for her voice was already
flooding in me as I became water,
air, light and shade.
        I cannot say whose soul
is here, whose breath is pressed
to the late winter light, breathless
in the blaze of a bare branch
and the silence
that breaks open the violets.

UNLOST

The page lifted
but *there is no book*
just a breeze under my coat
& a swan wing dipped into the water
making a lustrous trail

Sitting beside you, after we just met
I was holding your book
and my name is written in it
one of the many—

passes through as on the pond shore
between blond stalks

AUGUST MY BODY

August is my body strewn with pinecones.

Sun dapples my forest feet.

Having no toes, I can't walk to the water.

The mossy trunk sinks into my skin after so many years.

All the brown hairs I've shed!

Fallen one by one, each carries a scent now woven through many vessels and breezes.

Naked, my life will be put to the notes of cricket wings.

A NEW LANDING

Inside every crustacean is a pillow
on a seabed made of sunrises.
As the ocean unrolls
the crustacean may find itself part
of a lyrical movement
that forms the damask
of the forest no one has ever seen
wherever we may land.

THE SPEECH OF TREES

The trees speak a language I haven't learned,
        I haven't learned the route their shadows take.

Their shadows that take me alone,
        alone in a body with no other shelter.

No shelter but shadows above and beneath,
        beneath limbs that can't grasp what is missing.

But the missing has given me longings,
        relentless longings that come from a place,

a place beyond these trees out my window,
        these trees out my window that never leave.

They never leave my days or my nights.
        And the days and nights fill them with wind,

a wind so strong there is nothing else.
        There is nothing else.

WALKING THROUGH A PAINTING
BY JOHN BIANCHI

If we comprehend it, it is not God

St Augustine of Hippo

The Housatonic

There, among the blue ranges that rise
to a pale apricot sky, I enter by
the house that stands among
a copse of birch trees. Their bark
is so bright! Not far from the two
fisherman talking by the shore.
Though I can't hear their words, one
holds out his arm to the lake, while
in his other hand he holds a net.
Moving forward, I can almost hear
the one humming as he stands up in the canoe
pulled to the shore, while the other
sitting quietly in front, stares at the house.
Now I'm at the curve in the rutted road
by the puddle in the shape of a gull
or angel, breathing to the others
like swans flying over us.
Our blood turns to water,
while the house will always be
with its door barely a smudge,
the reddish wall whose opening
lights the grass on the other side,
and the pink flowers still outside the fence
as grains rise from the cracks.

A PETAL IN ARKANSAS

My first petal of the season.
What a feeling
to touch it with my lip

as I pause on the pavement by a porch
where red, blue & yellow birds
made of wood sit inside
an old-fashioned bird cage.

True they can't sing, and one
of the bluebirds dangling
from a fishing line
itself dangles a spider thread,

and that broken thread
appears to be conducting
the twitter of a brown leaf
in the rusted birdbath
where the cage is perched.

How many worlds breathe
behind the curtains, the screens, the bars
of other cages, in cells & under eyelids,
humming as someone awakens
and another dies.

What else, who else is conducting
but part of the ceremony
where everyone plays a most humble
decisive note?

Someone is lifting the shade.
A white cat at a window.
A lustrous breeze brings
more petals down.

ELEGY TO A DANCER

I have been so fractured, so multiple & dazzling…
Lynda Hull

Through the window a sliver of light on my arm,
a feeling of vertigo from a dream of you alive
after all these years, wearing your sleek black dress
with the low neck. We were walking past
shop windows, arms linked, your bony back
straight as the monument we once climbed
whose stairway wound around a center space,
your pale-freckled arms smooth as a young girl's
in a dance that spun us together so briefly.

ON HAUNTED LAKE

This early morning I want
to tell you how the mist on the lake
looks like dancers without feet
whose wraithlike arms
weave and unweave
as if they're embracing
whatever they can
whirling like dervishes in their
deathless dance interlocked
with whoever has stepped
from the world—like the lovers
still holding hands through the air
after jumping from the towers,
clasping to their power
as their bodies faded,
their cries muted,
their souls rising
to see their own
selves amid the droplets of light
opening above water
that remembers everything.

At dawn in the lake mist
I see you dancing
in line with the others,
your arms wraithlike,
weaving and unweaving
as if to embrace
whatever you can—
dancing without feet,
whirling like a dervish,
you who just days ago
lay in bed yellow and splayed,

your shoulder bones whittled
to points, while your ribs
seemed to ripple, brother
who always had words
but could no longer talk,
your eyes slits of light,
your hand growing cool, your soul
spinning elsewhere by then—

knowing how passion
fuses us and burns us
to freefall somewhere on a lake
to the cry of a loon.

BEECH IN THE PUBLIC GARDEN

Its winter branches
hold the color of iron
only softer, the smooth limbs
spread wide. What would it be
to stand in one place
for a lifetime? So many breaths
rise through its branches.
And those names cut into the base—
whoever carved them
in some attempt to press
their mark into this world
where every fold and groove
trace memories and dreams
that have no setting.

IN A MINOR KEY

As Queen Anne's lace stirs
in a late summer breeze
along one side of the road,
each petal on the wheel
opens its cup to the wind,
and the green nests
of the not-yet-bloomed
cling to their weave
around this secret emptiness
whose breath only seems
still and dark,
while on the other side
of the road blond weeds
ripple and stream.

TO A FURTHER BLOSSOMING

Along a narrow uneven trail in a clearing
above a school, I heard in a creak
a human cry. The tree was dead.
A dead oaktree with a hollow
halfway up, places where the rough
gray bark looked eaten away, other
places raw, lichen pale, spongy
and bare. With broken limbs
drawn upward. From a distance
in the late light, it looked like
a jaggedly splayed, coal-colored
bouquet against the sky. A haunted,
haunting thing. But up close, its pulp
felt soft as velvet in my hand.
It wasn't so much a cry as a sigh
that someone had come to see
into its deepened space
what was not done blossoming.
The crumble of its rain-soaked,
drying wood had a milky-caramel
hue, while the black gash
in its chest made it humble
as my father with his open
wound I had to dress for months
before he died. Somehow, he appeared
to belong then, not to any earth
but past some distant peak or star, reaching
where he had not yet learned—
My teacher, you've been sculpted
by the wind as much as by the night
and windless unseen light
that opens us within. And here
you take me into your broken arms.

CURRENT

Your breath went to the cries
of geese, mourning dove, nuthatch,
and the wind riffling the pond.

I remember your eyes
that seemed to radiate
something immutable in the moments
just as they leave us.

How many stars I cannot see,
voices I cannot hear
that surround and penetrate
what falls through the branches

and rises through the roots
to the birdsong and breeze
by the pond edge at daybreak.

IV

Where are you lying
secret of the world
with so strong an odor?

Jean Follain, translated by W.S. Merwin

We are born to make one another sing.

C.D. Wright

THE ROCK OF DAVID

He appears translucent, looming over us
as the eyes look off, almost in two
directions. The hands different sizes,
while the smaller one holds a rock
whose inside we can't see
made of the same piece of marble
he is made of, all the roughness
smoothed in synchrony, but what
has been discarded? Another sculptor
threw away the hunk of marble
that Michelangelo found
to make this David. Parts of the original stone
are what the eyes are searching for
that the left hand clutches, a kind of hope
for a glimpse of what's locked
within the massive and the rough,
beyond knowing that we are always
seeking, impeded by fear when we clutch
something cold and hard in place of the light
that has no age. The rock is empty
and filled with the hopes of all
who imagine what it contains.

IS THAT A GOD YOU ARE SPEAKING TO?

What lies inside the black rectangular
box in your hands that you tap
to its hymn with your thumbs,
You cross the street near the Forum
without seeing me watching.
And that white vegetable in your ear—
not wood or stone—that makes you
laugh to the invisible?
When we worked in the catacombs
digging till our fingers bled,
we could only whisper as we scraped
to make shelves for the dead.
All we knew was that we too
would dissolve in the lava and mold.
Still we painted the fish, the good shepherd,
the winged anchor of hope
in the galleries and grit, praying
the newborns would somehow
be warmed in their shrouds.
What do you pray
while your thumbs dance?
The light was faint.
But the one working beside me
had blood I could feel in the damp
of that earth. Today on the roads
I would perish alone out of earth.

DEAR VITTORIA COLONNA,

when you compared yourself to a ravenous bird
that longed to both fly and be sheltered
by its mother's wings,
who tried to sing
what you couldn't release in words,
I understood it was at the tip of a branch
of God light *half-glimpsed*
from the hollow of that nest.
So briefly it blazes
to illuminate each page.
As if the bird opens its wings
to lighten its bones
and the vellum on which you wrote
your poem to Michelangelo
were marble and the rivers
of every wind could be still.

OF UNKNOWN VALUE

Everything happens at a cost. Time continues
without a price. I don't know why I dreamt
of a natural pool at the entrance to our driveway.
I was sitting on a rock in the middle of the pool
carved by ancient waters. But the capacity to dream
is cut by the necessity of waking to the unearthly
whiteness of moonlight on my hand, or the lowing
of an early morning owl. That's when I think
the world is nothing but language or metaphor
for navigating the warrens of a universal mind.
A thought evaporates, continuing on
in another form. Only something remains, perhaps
an ache or twinge down below from the cord
that can't separate itself from the body we love,
and the slim choice of words we have
disappears when the eyes open and the dream
stays scenic, despite all that has happened
to bulldoze it. A rabbit hops along
freezing at a human presence. It has no
definition, no address, no one to ask
if it's true. I saw my friends but couldn't
tell you their names or how I knew them.
They were swimming and looked so happy.

THE SCENT

The heart's fingerprints are everywhere.
                                    Richard Jackson

From somewhere in the city
come the colorful pungency
of oils and spices,
the scent of wet stone,
a woman perspiring
in her high heels that click by,
and the smoke a squinty-eyed man
exhales as he taps
his ashes to the ground
a few feet from the doorway
where a raw-cheeked woman sleeps
under a blanket of particles
near a piece of mooncake some pigeons
& sparrows are sharing.

SOFTLY WOVEN THING

It looked like a feathery clump
or thatch of a paw, this tuft
caught on a dried yellow weed tip.

Bending down to the sandy ground,
I touched the strands
that slightly fluttered.

Maybe this came from a plant,
with the rest blown away.

One part was free,
and one torn, perhaps grieving
for the rest
scattered across the earth
and beyond, held together as we are
by forces of unknown measure.

PAPER ANGEL

On my wall, your wings appear
as petals of flame.
The patina of teardrops.
Between them
in the blue space at the chest
a sparkling grain.

This gift I can't hold in my hand.

Out the window, called the brightest
of stars, Venus is not a star,
but an eye
that looks on, filling us
with an explicable radiance.

From Venus we're smaller than any crystal.

All the suffering all over the earth
has made that crystal.

You hold in your heart a grain of light.
From what sea or flower or voice
am I too filled?

Who touches me in my endless place.

EPISTLE TO THE LATE FALL WEEDS

At dawn you glow,
along with the stones in the dirt road.
Each hollow seed is

a soul partly returned
from the other side.

I can't know
each of your lives
any more than I can know mine.

At the pond my shadow disappears.

I wait for another life
to grow from this one,
watching you lightly sway
as the ducks take off

disheveling the water and spreading it
in soundless tones
that call our lost shadows home.

WITHOUT A WORD

Reflected on the window
a few book spines silver
along the forest edge

there's a face made of light

a thin shadow crosses the cheek
outlined in light on the glass

from an opening in the forest

I cannot take my eyes away
or rise from the chair
tied to this thread

whose face holds such peace

love beyond any word

saturated with light
gathers me

FOUND AMONG THE LOST

Not my glove, but my empty hand.
Not my empty hand, but the opening
in a pocket where the chill slips through.

A ring, a necklace with its gold
medallion, the last watch
my grandfather bought me, my grandmother without
saying goodbye.

Papers recording the passages
of those I loved. Papers that crumble
at a touch found
in the drawer of a forgotten desk.

Beside a bench in the cemetery, among
the patches of moss, white violets. A flutter
without a voice or name—

Not bewilderment,
but breath of the wounded, unrequited,
rising. Not lost, but given the scent
of what blossoms.

A corner where one can come
and go. Places for the soul to lie down
and be gathered.

SOMEONE LEFT THE WINDOWS OPEN

I can't close the immense
windows of the ancient theater,
or the eyes of the stone angel
that stares past me,
or the space between pillars.

When I come to the river
I gaze at the white rivulets, wondering
what they are saying.

The white-limbed leafless
sycamores that line the banks
barely sway, as all
of the life and love I have known
will be forgotten.

THE WAY OF LEAVES

The leaves hang together,
but each falls alone.

Yesterday a leaf
fell among many, unheard.

While it was falling
it swayed—for that moment.

Somewhere now
a leaf lets go.

And another, one
by one all over the world,

leaving the same color stain,
the same earth scent,

the same wordless lament
for their passage.

VILLAGE

Heaven's in the voices.
Anne Marie Macari

Whatever is hushed comes
to light these chimes out my window
with a slight breath, to make them
ever so lightly clink, reminding me
of the bells of the village
where I once lived, now drowned out
by this windy night.

Some say the soul fleeing destruction
leaves the body
just before it's time.

In the ringing, such tones
whose names are forgotten,
released of all longing. Whatever it is
that separates us fades away.

Notes

"Carrying the Abyss": "When a young dreamer lay dying in his sleeping bag…" refers to Christopher McCandless who disappeared in the Alaska wilderness in 1992 and whose story is told in Jon Krakauer's *Into the Wild*.

"From a Bench on a Hill": Some of the details I allude to are found in *Rombo* by Esther Kinsky, Fitzcarraldo Editions, 2022.

"Lessening": "The soul barks, the soul meows" is a line from a poem by Linda Gregg in *All of it Singing*.

"Unlost": Italicized lines are from the poem "Ikon" in *Door in the Mountain* by Jean Valentine.

"How Many are Buried in Unmarked Graves": In the then Soviet Union in the 1960s to 80s in a popular game called *Sekretiki* ("little secrets") children buried candy wrappers and other things under pieces of broken glass to make pictures only special friends might see.

"Current": "just as they leave us" is a line in a poem by W.S. Merwin.

Acknowledgments

Grateful acknowledgment is made to the following publications in whose pages these poems first appeared, sometimes in earlier versions:

Avatar Review: "Lessening," "August My Body"

Bluebird Wood: "The Scent"

E-merge: "His Sign Asks for Water" (Woody Barlow Prize), "To a Further Blossoming," "A Petal in Arkansas"

Lily Poetry Review: "Shadow of the Untouchable," "Marking the Place"

On the Seawall: "Refuge"

Paddleshots: "To the Wind"

Poetry Miscellany: "Cloudscape"

Solstice: "The Fog is Adrift," "Carrying My Abyss (I Sally Forth)"

The Citron Review: "In a Minor Key"

The Poetry Porch: "A Forest Remnant," "The Speech of Trees," "Voices in Leaves," "Beech in the Public Garden," "The Way of Leaves,' "(The) Current," "Patch of Woods," "Is That a God You are Speaking to?," "From a Bench on a Hill (Questions for a Bench on a Hill)," "Elegy to a Scrap"

2River: "Epistle to the Late Fall Weeds," "Found Among the Lost"

I am grateful to Petra Breen, Deborah Brown, Miriam Drev, Mary Kane, Ana Jelnikar, Nancy Lagomarsino, Lynn Levin, Miriam O'Neal, Dzvinia Orlowsky, Maggie Paul, Susan Thomas, Scott Withiam, the River Pretty Writers' community and the Press 53 workshop group for their friendship, camaraderie and insights. Thanks to Annie Newcomer for her generosity and friendship, and for introducing me to Dairy Hollow Writers' Retreat. Many thanks to Rick Jackson for his editorial vision. Much thanks to Richard Hoffman, Annie Marie Macari and Betsy Sholl for their support. Profound gratitude to Eileen Cleary for giving this book a home and to Christine Jones and the rest of the Lily team who helped make it a reality.

About the Author

Barbara Siegel Carlson's previous books are *What Drifted Here* (Cherry Grove 2023), *Once in Every Language* (Kelsay Books 2017) and *Fire Road* (Dream Horse Press 2013). She co-translated with Ana Jelnikar *Look Back, Look Ahead, Selected Poems of Srečko Kosovel.* Her poems, translations and articles have been published in the US and abroad. Her poetry has been nominated for Best of the Net and the Pushcart Prize. Carlson is a Poetry in Translation Editor of *Solstice: A Magazine of Diverse Voices.* She lives in Carver, Massachusetts.